The Language of Light

poems of wit, whimsy, and (maybe) wisdom

Nancy Thomas

The Language of Light

©2024 by Nancy Thomas

Fernwood Press
Newberg, Oregon
www.fernwoodpress.com

All rights reserved. No part may be reproduced
for any commercial purpose by any method without
permission in writing from the copyright holder.

Printed in the United States of America

Cover and page design: Mareesa Fawver Moss

Cover image: Aaron Burden

Author photo: Ron Dingman

ISBN 978-1-59498-142-5

*Thank God for girlfriends
who over time and distance
have sustained me, prayed with me,
and made me laugh.*

*To
Anita Aylard
Diane Bradley
Elaine Cammack
Susan Espejo
Ruth Galeb
Darlene Graves
Mary Thiessen-Nation
Catherine Treziack*

> You must never stop being whimsical.
> —Mary Oliver

> I do rather squirm at the awful picture of a very minor poet taking [her]self with dreadful solemnity.
> —Charles Williams

Pacifist Poet

William Stafford, sweet poet,
said that one in every ten poems
he wrote was good enough for publication.
That encourages me
'cause I write a lot of bad poems.
But, like Stafford, I'm a pacifist.
I don't kill any of my poems.
For the nine poor poems
I find a comfortable spot,
lay them down, and let them sleep.
You get to read the tenth poem.
Lucky you.

Contents

Pacifist Poet 5
Introduction 11
A Way with Words 15
   You Have a Way with Words 16
   I'm Good with Languages 17
   A Word Like *Lugubrious* 18
   Why I Never Use the Word *Plethora* 19
   Short Poems on Particle Physics 20
   No Experts at Home Here 22
   A Short Poem on Anatomy 22
   Car Trouble 22
   With a Name like Weasel 23
   Qualms 24
   The Creeps 25
   The Ultimate Bull 26
   A Quaker Lady Learns to Swear 27
   Grammatical Violence 28
   A Whole Nother 28
   Bilingualism 29
   Challenged 29
   Odebolt 30
   A Tale of Two Cows 31

    The Mature Poet Takes a Walk in the Woods 32
    Come to Your Senses, Nancy 33
    God's Poem 35
    Sometimes Understatement Doesn't Work............... 39

Uncertain Terms 41
    Uncertain Terms 42
    Eating My Words 43
    The Pregnant Pause 44
    Bare Naked.. 44
    Fat Chance 45
    Going Dutch 46
    The Naked Eye... 47
    In Answer to Your Question 48
    Food for Thought 49
    My Bad 49
    American Monsters.. 50
    Medical Breakthrough 52
    The Turnip 53
    There Were Five of Them 54
    In the Nick of Time... 55
    Body Shop: Parts and Replacements....................... 56
    Seven Views of a Rabbit Trail 57

Conversations with Hal
and Other Peculiar People 59
    Worshipping the Squirrel... 60
    Our Life in Pennsylvania:
        Questions and Answers 61
    The List of Perils Grows... 62
    My Husband Compliments Me.................................. 63
    A Reassurance to My Husband
        Who Sometimes Gets Kicked in Bed 63
    A Comment to My Husband
        Who Tends to Let His
        Yes Be Yes and His No, No 63

Andrea	64
God and Cats	65
Peter Wonders about Death and Other Stuff	66
Trout Tickling	68
No Survivors	69
Old Testament War Revised	70
The Wedding Gift	71
Course Correction?	72
What?	73
Strangely Appropriate	74
CEO	75
Little Children Know	76
Such Friends	77
Verbal Rewards	78
Saint Paul Meets a Quaker Lady	78
Clay Pot	79
Just Asking	81
Offensive	82
A Word from Grandma	83
Trail Guide	84
Life in an Old Growth Forest	85
Are We Old Yet?	86
Who Done It?	88
Old Romance	88
Told to Me at Lunch	89
Unacquainted	89
Tact	90
Over by the Creek	91
Skimpy Blessing	92
Three Conversations in the Exercise Room	93
Goodbye	96
Hal, at 76	96
In that Very Instant	97
How I Am	98

A Brief Poetic Treatise on Fine Cuisine	99
It Had To Be Done	100
Just a Tweak	101
At the Beginning of Another Grim Day	103
Over the River and through the Woods	104
Crowded, but Green	105
Bird-napping: The Secret of Old Age	106
Ancient Blessing	107
The Temple Ages	108
Devotions	108
In the Fullness of Time	109
Title Index	111
First Line Index	117

Introduction

American poet John Updike divided his poetry into two categories: light verse and real poetry. He described light verse as "a kind of cartooning with words," while the serious stuff deals with substance and reality. He admitted that the division between the two wiggled.

I admire Updike's poetry, but his categories make me squirm and wiggle. I imagine if he read this book, he'd label most of it "light." I resent that, which is silly.

I like to think that humorous poems, even whimsical stuff, are still poetry. Real poetry. I've chosen to use the word *light* in the title, but this only superficially refers to Updike's category. It's a recognition that humor produces a certain lightness of spirit. Laughter lifts us up and gives a more gracious perspective of reality. Humor can also turn stuff on its head, helping us see people/problems/culture (especially our own culture) from a different viewpoint.

I have one more reason I use the word *light*, and that's in the sense of illumination. Often laughter precedes insight. I hope some of the poems in this book do that.

The other word I employ in the title is *language*. I love language in general. This book of poems celebrates language, especially the English language.

A few years back, at an intercultural poetry reading, a man from the audience challenged me: "Aren't you frustrated at having to write your poetry in English?" he asked. "Such a harsh, irregular language. Spanish, on the other hand, is lyrical, sensual, musical, and more logical than English. And the sounds match the letters."

He had a point, but he had missed several others. I sensed his question was more than rhetorical so I responded as kindly yet as honestly as I could:

I've listened to you and others for whom English is a second language, and you're right. The language is unsuited to poetry. The English taught in countries around the world is valid for business, industry, academics, or medicine. Many of those studying want to migrate to the US and make money. That English, however, doesn't make poems.

You're also right about the irregularities of English, a great frustration to learners. Coming from so many cultural roots, borrowing from such a multitude of languages, it does seem like a mongrel tongue.

That's one of the reasons I love it. Those who live the English language at a deep level, experience its twists, contradictions, impossible puzzles, and incredible variety as a delight, a playground of words.

Poetry in Spanish, Arabic, or Japanese is often beautiful, lyrical, following the logic of its language. It's like walking in a sunlit garden. The splendor of the flowers, laid out in orderly beds, overwhelms. The paths curve and meander in expected, or unexpected, ways. If one gets lost, it's likely because of the beauty, not the lack of order. The paths eventually lead home. There are poems for the picking.

Writing poems in English is taking a hike in the wilderness. I may begin on a trail, but it soon peters out among the scrub brush and high altitude keswara trees. The upward climb challenges my strength and energy. Deep chasms surprise the unwary. Danger lurks. But condors and eagles soar overhead, and tiny alpine flowers peek out in more varieties than I knew existed. As I approach the glaciers, poems are hiding everywhere.

I've divided this book into four sections. The first, "A Way with Words," celebrates different aspects of language—its sounds, grammar, quirks, and all that words can, or can't, do. The second section, "Uncertain Terms," deals with common figures of speech in the English language, metaphors we take for granted, but which confuse my literally-minded autistic grandson. The third section, "Conversations with Hal and Other Peculiar People," focuses on human relationships and includes insights from scripture. Finally, the fourth section, "Life in an Old Growth Forest," is my attempt to approach growing older with courage and humor; many of these poems reflect life in a retirement community.

Feel free to smile, laugh, or groan. I pray you'll also spy grace hiding in the silences between the words.

A Way with Words

You Have a Way with Words,

Grandma, she told me.
I wondered what that meant.
Sometimes words
hack through the weeds
in the mind
to bring clarity.
Sometimes words make a way.
Sometimes they don't.
Sometimes words
get in the way.
Sometimes they ping
off the floor, ricochet
from wall to ceiling,
popping and cackling
as they go, and I long
for sweet silence.
Those times I say to myself,
Away with words!
Away with words!

Maybe that's what
she meant.

I'm Good with Languages

This morning on the path to the beach
the wind whistled through the scrub brush
and I answered back in the vernacular.
The ocean, unusually talkative,
threw waves and words on the shore.
I understood her perfectly.
Two sea gulls bandied a joke back and forth
in their dialect. I got it. Laughed out loud.
And while the rising sun chose to be silent,
I knew what he meant to say.

A Word Like *Lugubrious*

needs a poem of its own.
Consider the slime and the slink of it,
the slightly sinister wink of its eye
as it peeks from behind potted plants at wakes,
lingers at the altars of Protestant revivals,
or sobs with soap opera heroines.
An irreverent Uriah Heapish word,
a marbles-in-the-mouth sound,
it offers no apologies
for its lumpish singularity.

Some suggestions for everyday use:
—*This piano is lugubriously out of tune.*
—*He shed a lugubrious tear*
     as she passed him the marmalade.
—*This morning at exactly 5:37,*
     a lugubrious lummox was sighted
     at the corner of 11th and Lucerne
     in downtown LA. We have investigators
     on the scene and will interrupt our broadcast
     to bring up-to-date coverage
     on this fast-breaking story.
—*Not tonight, dear. I'm feeling lugubrious.*

Why I Never Use the Word *Plethora*

—It wears rhinestone earrings.
—It goes to academic lectures in lime-green satin shoes with pointed toes and spiked heels.
—It speaks with a French accent but has never been to France.
—It hangs out with words like *felicitous* and *vacuous*.
—It thinketh more highly of itself than it ought.

Common sense dictates that I keep my distance.

Short Poems on Particle Physics
(based on a DVD class)

Take the neutrino,
a weak force that is completely bizarre.
It has no mass, no charge,
but it spins and cruises through matter
without so much as a by-your-leave.
It is, says the professor,
the most esoteric, wispy, ghost-like particle there is.
Coming directly from the center of the sun,
it invades downward through the roof
and upward through the floor
of Friendsview Manor, where I happen to live,
to bombard my body at the rate
of 100 billion neutrinos per square centimeter per
 second.

No wonder I feel so tired.

* * * *

And then there's the Higgs boson particle
and the Higgs boson field that permeates space.
It's apparently massive and is responsible for symmetry
 breaking.
I guess it's good to know who—or what—to blame.
But, as our professor assures us, *Symmetry breaking is good.*
The world is boring when things are perfectly symmetrical.

* * * *

I've learned
that there is a strong force and a weak force,
that *the strong force produces total strangeness,*

while *the weak force has a history of being weird.*
I believe both statements but remain uncertain
about the difference between "strange" and "weird."

* * * *

You can create something out of nothing, claims the professor,
speaking of particle production in an accelerator,
but only for a really short time.

* * * *

Quarks, the professor assures us,
are as real as Pluto.
I'm sure he means the planet,
but the floppy-eared Disney hound pops into my brain.
It doesn't matter; both are real,
so I guess quarks are, too.

* * * *

To step into the future, we now have a big TOE—
a "Theory Of Everything."
That's not as arrogant as it sounds,
but rather a hope of one day discovering at the simplest level
what ties all life together.
He sums up the class by telling us the Big Idea behind it all—
that *the world is orderly.*
I suspected as much.

No Experts at Home Here

Please, whatever you say
about me, don't call me
an expert. Ugly word.
I'd much rather be known
as a current-spert,
and I'm iffy about
that one.

A Short Poem on Anatomy

I never met a tarsal
I didn't like.
There's some mighty fine
tarsals out there.

Car Trouble

*(on hearing my grandson complain
that the donuts in his car have failed)*

The donuts in my new car are fine,
but the biscuits are shot.

With a Name like Weasel

how could he not
have a mean lean body,
tiny nails for fingers,
and gums sprouting
pointy teeth.
His grin alone
makes field mice tremble.
Whoever named this elongated
rat must draw his words
from a deep well of malice.
The poor beast
doesn't stand a chance.

Qualms

While poor in the goods
of this world, I am rich
in qualms. Not just two or three,
I possess dozens of these emotive
creatures that stream in my blood
and settle in my stomach.
As they dog-paddle in the juices
they talk to me. They whisper,
warn. Sometimes they play
Holy Ghost, and sometimes
I let them. My fashion qualms
inform me that my brown socks
offend my black pants.
Shut up, I tell them.
My moral qualms tell me
it's a lie to answer *Fine, thank you*
to a rhetorical greeting when
in fact I feel lousy. And now
my citizenship qualms insist
that although the next four
years may be hellish, I am
to behave with propriety, salute
the flag, support the troops,
and not even dream of marching
in the streets. Silly qualms.

The Creeps

Whenever he appears on the screen
and opens his mouth,
I get the creeps.
Not fear, panic, irritation,
butterflies, discomfort, or even the willies.
It's the creeps, I tell you.
They start at the ends of my toes and fingers,
gradually crawl up my legs and arms,
hit my trunk, work their insidious way
up my neck, chin, eyebrows;
boggle my brain; sliver my soul.

In time, Anchor Person smiles
and says, *That's it for now, folks!*
We'll see you again tomorrow night.
Same time. Same station.
I'm left with these gaping wounds,
aftermath of the nightly creeps
and the evening news.

The Ultimate Bull

*This meat came
from the ultimate bull,*
she warned us as we sat
down to Sunday dinner.
Fireplace heat
warmed the room as outside
temperatures dipped
to the low twenties, belying
sun that streamed
through bare branches.
*He was the last of the herd,
and we probably waited
too long to kill him.
Actually it's T-bone. It
looks like pieces of roast
because we had to
reprocess it.*
Tough but tasty, we put
the old beast to his final rest.
After dinner we sat
around the table,
told stories, cracked
pistachios, chuckled
at old jokes.
Later the evening news—
impeachment, the Speaker's resignation,
collateral damage in Iraq, Monica,
and President Clinton, teary eyed,
saying, *I can't begin to tell you
how sorry I am.*

A Quaker Lady Learns to Swear

You need to learn to swear,
he tells me.
A Quaker like you,
so controlled—
it's not healthy.

I wonder if he might be right.
I do feel pressed down at times
by the undone dishes and frayed edges,
not to mention the major injustices of life.

Leaning into memory, I bring up
words from TV and novels, phrases
my grandfather used when provoked.
I rehearse them mentally,
avoiding the mirror.

A few weeks later,
something he says
(I can't remember what),
—a twist of sarcasm, a patronizing hint—
and a voice whispers, *Now.*
I look straight at him
and with a keen but measured ferocity say,
I just don't give a hell.

In the following silence, I realize
I haven't quite pulled it off.
Finally he says, *If you're going to swear,*
at least do it right.

Warning: I'm practicing.
Next time I'll get it.
Mountains will quake.

Grammatical Violence

Although a Quaker,
I am violent when it comes to infinitives.
Ever since my grammar school teacher
told me I could never, under any circumstances,
split an infinitive, I said to myself,
Oh yeah? I determined to gleefully split
away, no matter the rules. Ever afterward,
I'm pleased to proudly say,
I hack away at those pesky infinitives
without shame or regret.

A Whole Nother

If you're going to give me a nother,
give me a whole nother.
No partial notions,
no half-baked little clones of the real thing.
It's either the whole ball of wax,
or nothing at all,
thank you very much.

Bilingualism

If I tease someone in English
I'm pulling his leg.
In Spanish, however,
if my friend teases me,
he leaves my limbs alone
and yanks on my hair,
as in ¡*Me estás tomando el pelo!*
In order to encourage
bilingual multiculturalism,
important for world peace,
all one has to do is tease
a man with a hairy leg.

Challenged

I am linguistically challenged
when it comes to spelling.
As much as I love the English language,
its orthography baffles.
Take for instance the difference
between *desert* and *dessert*.
I can't keep them straight,
as many times as I consult Mr. Webster.
So please don't hold it against me
if some evening, after the main course,
I serve you frosted cactus
sprinkled with sand
along with tumbleweed tea.

Odebolt

I spent the years of my infancy and childhood
in Odebolt, Iowa. Small then, now it boasts
upward of 915 people. I wonder about the etymology
of the funny name. Wikipedia claims it may have come
from one Odebeau, a French trapper
who may or may not have been historical.
I like to think my hometown was named for Odin,
the one-eyed Norse god of war (who was also, ironically,
the god of poets). I imagine him with a lightning bolt
in hand, ready for battle. Odin. Bolt. Odebolt.
My question is whether Odebolt
was his base, the place he stood
when he launched his bolts,
or if it was his target?
This makes a difference
in how I understand
my life story.

A Tale of Two Cows

> "Glory be to God for dappled things,
> For skies of couple-color as a brinded cow."
> —Gerard Manley Hopkins

I stood at the window last evening,
marveling at a cloud-streaked sky.
Oranges and purples stretched and shifted
in lines and clumps, strange and counter,
when I saw him—Gerard Manley Hopkins's cow
up there in the stratosphere, most definitely brinded.
He seemed to float along for the longest time
grazing on the clouds. Slowly the scene
dimmed and faded. Night came on.

Sometime later, I looked out
to admire the half-moon, dappled and spotted,
but still adazzle, when I saw a shadow invade its surface
from below, then race up over the top and away.
With sudden revelation, I understood that they were one
and the same, that Hopkins's sky-cow was the same cow-
that-jumped-over-the-moon I had known as a child.
I swear it. The very same.

The Mature Poet Takes a Walk in the Woods

"Immature poets imitate; mature poets steal."
–T.S. Eliot

Whose woods these are
I think I know
but I'm not altogether certain
and will therefore
try to be discrete.

It's getting harder to see the path
with all this fog coming in on little cat feet,
but, after all, we learn by going
where we have to go.

And, it has to be said,
these woods are lovely,
dark and deep
and I do so love hiking.
I'm sure I'll come out of them
in due time and go gently
home into that good night.

Come to Your Senses, Nancy

he says
so I do

I approach sight first
head on, face to face
and thank you
I say
for orange sunsets
that field of Queen Anne's Lace
the irony in my father's eyes
without you
I say
what would I know

I approach sound sideways
sidling up slowly
so as not to startle
and thank you to you too
I say
for Brahm's First
and Splish Splash I Was Takin' a Bath
for the rain in the trees
and the traffic off Highway 10
that I pretended was ocean surf
without you
life would be bland

I come to taste bit by bit
biting the apple
remembering salt on the tongue
rain under the trees, face up, mouth open
taffy and slow kisses
coffee to help me greet each day

thank you
I say
for waking me up

Smell is the little sister
I sometimes think I could
do without
but thank you anyway
I say
for honeysuckle
and the short-lived lilac
for coffee again
and the trees just after the rain
don't go
I tell her
it's better with you here

I come to touch
forever needy
never seeming to get enough
thank you
I say
for remembered embraces
slaps on the back
sitting in my mother's lap
petting my collie
my hands cupping a scratchy chin
stay
I say

I come,
a grateful beggar in a hard time,
to my senses

God's Poem

> *We are God's poem, created in Christ Jesus*
> *for the good works he planned for us from*
> *before the foundation of the earth.*
> *—Ephesians 2:10*

If you can believe that
you're already on the way
to becoming part of the poem.

***

"Good for nothing,"
my grandfather teased me.
He was a wise man.
Good poems are always
free for the picking.

***

Like a cheerful giver,
God loveth
a silly poet.

***

Wisdom and whimsy
hold hands,
opposites who attract.

***

The Word made flesh
fleshes out in words
that tumble
in the winds of grace.

***

Living poems
usually have
surprise endings.

***

A tumbleweed,
the poem gathers and grows,
bounds
across the prairie,
playing its way
into heaven.

***

Read the poem slowly.
Consider the silences
between the words.

***

Some keep strict time
and rhyme; some
bounce to an irregular
but discernible rhythm;
some are free verse.
God writes us all,
includes us in his repertoire.

***

Salt, leaven, light, seed.
We are his metaphors,
grace-gifts
to the world.

***

This library
is open to the public,
no admission fee,
no check-out limits,
no late-book fines.
Read us here
or take us home.

***

Some of us
are harder to read
than others.

***

Some poems have a short fuse.
Others yield their fire
slowly and only
to those who hold them
in the palm of their hand,
open to the sun.

***

This is no vanity press.
The poems are free
but come at great cost.

***

Be still
and let it
grow.

Sometimes Understatement Doesn't Work

Be wary of the exclamation point
the writing gurus tell us.
Let the words speak for themselves.
Your readers aren't dim.
If you craft your work
they'll know when to smile
gasp cry or rage.

But last night's sunset
totally did me in.
When I tried to describe it
all I could say was

!
!! !! !
!!!!!!!!!! !!!!!!!!
!!!
!!!!!!!!!!!!!!!!!!!!!!!!!!!!!!!!!
!!!!!!!!!!!!!!!!!!!!!!
!!!
!

Uncertain Terms

Uncertain Terms

*I will continue to say
this in no uncertain terms,*
said the Man in the Meeting
without literally pounding
the pulpit. I sat there, silent
as usual, and wondered if
it were possible to find any
term that is not uncertain.
Given the nature of language,
the propensity of words
to wiggle and the vicissitudes
of the human beings that use
those words, could there
even exist—anywhere—a
certain term? Perhaps a botanical
descriptor, like phylum
or photosynthesis, red
wood or rhododendron?
A specific color, burnt
umber, say, or periwinkle
blue? Or a place? Mt. Hood
is simply Mt. Hood, right?
No ands, ifs, or buts about
Mt. Hood, right? You're
either there or you're not.

But what happens if you find
yourself lost on Mt. Hood,
having passed bushes that may
or may not have been rhododendrons,
under a sky that is no longer
any shade of blue?
What then?

Eating My Words

*If it doesn't pan out exactly
as I've said*, I told him,
*I'll just have to eat
my words.*

The very next day, as a matter
of fact, I started in
on the nouns. I plopped them whole,
one at a time, in my mouth.
First I sucked the juice out,
then swallowed the pulp.
One caught in my throat
and I had to wash it down
with a few slurpy adjectives.

The verbs crunched and crackled
as my teeth bit down. I seasoned
them with some choice adverbs.

In a small gesture of rebellion
I saved the prepositions
for dessert. As any real chef
knows, you can't use a preposition
to end anything with, so that's exactly
what I did.

All in all, it was a most
satisfying meal.

The Pregnant Pause

hesitates before opening the door.
She knows it's time.
Summoning her courage
she turns the knob,
enters the house.
Her parents are waiting up
for her. She knew
they would. They sit
in the living room waiting
waiting for her to break
the pause, tell them
what they don't want to know.

Bare Naked

is a provocative name
for granola.
I sprinkle it over my yogurt—
plain, white, nondescript,
then add the plump, round
blueberries, enticing
to the taste buds.

There's more to good nutrition
than meets the eye.

Fat Chance

I've been known to take
all sorts of chances
and get away with it.
I took a romantic chance
once and it got me two kids
and seven grandkids.
Once I rode a chance
all the way to Istanbul
and I almost didn't want
to come home.
But the fat chance
eludes me. You'd think
its sloppy bulk would provide
a handhold or two.
But no. It slips
my grasp and scoots away
into the night every
time I come near.
Not for you, it seems to say.
Not now.
Not ever.

Going Dutch

Let's go Dutch, he said
and I said yes
so when he met me
at the door
I was ready,
a bunch of tulips
in hand,
shod in
wooden shoes.
I guess we
had a good time
other than
some awkwardness
paying the bill
but all I remember
now is my
aching feet.

The Naked Eye

I left my coat
at my uncle's house,
lost the left sock
in the laundry,
and outgrew
all the rest.
Damned growth spurt!
It left me
without covering,
exposed to the elements.
Not fair. My twin,
over there to my left,
is fully clothed
and frankly fancy,
from cocky French beret
to designer T-shirt,
skinny jeans, and sequined
cowboy boots.
She's more about being seen
than seeing.
And here am I. Bare.
But heed this warning.
Now, more than ever before,
I see you.

In Answer to Your Question

Yes, I used to put God
in a box, but it turned
out to be a Jack-
in-the box, and God
kept jumping out
and scaring me
at the most inconvenient
times. One day he
jumped all the way
out, leaving me
with this empty tin
cube, red paint peeling.
I finally threw it
away. God remains
at large.

Food for Thought

I'm told that fish is brain food.
In order to enhance clear thinking
and the ability to analyze and evaluate,
tuna sandwiches are really helpful.
But the idea of mackerel
swimming between my ears
and trout slurping around in the medulla
stops me short.
The barracuda, frankly,
gives me a headache.

My Bad

I shouldn't have said anything
but I did. I told the secret,
spoiled the surprise,
and paved a path for trouble.
I simultaneously
opened a can of cats
and let the worm out of the bag.
As if that were not enough,
the cats ate the worm
and proceeded to get sick
all over my carpet.
Will I ever learn?

American Monsters

1

Stiff but receptive, they wait for the rustling
to still. All fours planted firmly on the parquet

(not a hint of wobble), they survey the domain
over which they will soon take command.

Solid oak, this one, substantial, a Presence
to be reckoned with. At last, in the fullness of Time,

Chairperson leans into the Meeting, breathes Order,
and once again creates a World.

2

A vague but threatening
relational ooze,

Significant Other
seeps through our defenses

and gums up the shore line,
an emotional oil spill

that neutralizes wings
and turns song to a gurgle.

3

The archetypal beast from the sea
Anchor Person rises with monstrous regularity

each evening at 6:30 (EST)
trailing bad news like kelp,

pinging us with pellets of virtual reality
that zoom down the airwaves

and invade our homes
with a global stink.

4

Hear it? That creek of the floorboards,
that whisper in the dark? It comes stealthily,

rolling down the halls of academia
or floating at cerebral level.

Department Head, disembodied,
tentacled and tenured, directs brainwashing

operations with a grim solemnity, and the status
that seeps from his wounds is cosmic.

Medical Breakthrough

Here's good news for all
you sufferers of Restless Nostril Syndrome!
Lestiferitch (scientific name: acidilipoferous oxipilipoof)
is being widely hailed as a major
breakthrough, calming those wayward
nostril hairs and bringing peace of head.
Mr. Hector Bulgaria of Odebolt, Iowa
says, *Finally I can sleep through
the night without wind on my face.*
And Susan B. Queen of Ramona, California
testifies that *It's amazingly quick
and pain free. At last my nose is at rest.*

> [Warning: In some people Lestiferitch
> is reported to have transferred the restlessness
> from nostrils to toes, resulting in uncontrollable
> twitching throughout the night. In others
> it causes heart failure,
> loss of breath, or wildly exotic thoughts.
> A few have perished, but they
> are in the minority and the tests
> are nonconclusive.]

Ask your doctor if Lestiferitch is for you.

The Turnip

You can't squeeze blood from a turnip. –Folk proverb

It wasn't very appetizing, so
instead of eating it,
I grasped it between my hands,
held my breath,
and squeezed
until my face turned red,
squeezed for an eon of minutes,
squeezed until the fibers broke down
and the center collapsed,
squeezed and squeezed and squeezed
until all that was left
was a pittance of pulp
and a small pinkish puddle
of blood
on my plate.

There Were Five of Them

in the beginning.
They all started out little;
some of them grew.
#1 went to market.
He was the entrepreneurial pig,
the breadwinner,
the one who made the rules.
He grew big and was the first
to be slaughtered.
#2 stayed back
and tended the home fires.
She had a bow tied to her tail
and an inferiority complex
that quietly turned her bitter
over time.
#3 had roast beef.
A carnivore with sharp teeth,
what he lacked in wholesome humor
he made up in sarcasm.
#4 had none. It was not
that she didn't want any.
More that she repressed her
desires in a frigid asceticism.
She was by far the most
religious of the group.
#5 cried *wee wee wee*
all the way home.
A real whiner,
he was the only survivor.
No one bothered
to butcher him.

In the Nick of Time

I was a believer. I grew up
with a firm faith in the Tooth
Fairy, Jesus, and Santa Claus.
The grown-ups in my life
said it was so, and I believed
them. The Fairy left monetary
evidence, and the Sunday
school stories about Jesus
were too good not to be true.

While the logistics surrounding
Santa Claus puzzled—how
could he visit every
house in the world in a single
night and how could his sleigh
hold all that stuff?—I didn't let them
trouble me for long. After all,
he always showed up at *my*
house just in the nick of time
to make Christmas morning
magical. I asked for nothing
more.

Body Shop: Parts and Replacements

It's an American secret,
but every small town has one
lurking somewhere on Main Street
between Dunkin' Donuts and Ace Hardware—
the Body Shop. It's best to visit
in the light of day, never after dark.
A whiff of formaldehyde greets you
as you enter. Rows of shelves stretch
back, inviting exploration.
Bins of fingers (neatly sorted into thumbs,
indexes, pinkies, and such); tubs of toes;
noses of all sizes and shapes nudged into nooks;
crannies full of craniums. Whatever
you're missing or want to replace,
persistence and courage will lead you to it.
In the cold storage locker at the back
hide the vulnerable inner wonders—hearts,
kidneys, an esophagus or two. Shelves
of bottled body fluids beckon your perusal,
and from the ceiling dangle inflated bladders
and lungs, strange dark balloons.
If you wait until Black Friday
you can get two of whatever
for the price of one.
What a deal.

> [As a child I was frightened at seeing Body Shops on our family drives through small towns. I was actually too frightened to ask my parents about these places, so my childish imagination ran amok.]

Seven Views of a Rabbit Trail

1

Sometimes the path you were following
would have led you to sweeping vistas
of beauty and light, but now
you'll never know. All you see is grass.

2

The problem is there are so many of them.
Which, where, when, why?
The options distract.

3

Once a rabbit trail took me
to a chocolate-covered surprise—
the Easter Bunny herself!
I can't tell you how that made me feel.

4

Sometimes the diversion leads to something
better, becomes a clearer trail
to a more defined space. The blues
are bluer, the flowers more themselves,
the streams more musical.
You would never want to go back—

5

except you'll always wonder
what you missed.

6

The planned-on road
might have led to your true love
or the perfect job. It might have restored
your place in line. In time it might even
have taken you home.

7

Rabbit trails are not just for bunnies.
But humans, who are not as smart as rabbits,
had better be careful.

Conversations with Hal
and Other Peculiar People

Worshipping the Squirrel

As I walked in the room
I saw my husband down on his knees
in front of our wooden squirrel.
Are you worshipping that squirrel?
I demanded.
No, Nancy, he replied.
I'm looking for my glasses.
That seemed a plausible answer.
Looking-for-the-glasses is a game
he frequently plays.
Sooner or later they turn up
as they did this time,
with no help from the squirrel.

I must admit, however,
that the squirrel is fetching.
I find myself sometimes
gazing at his black marble eyes,
admiring the stiff flow of fir
on his upright tail,
sensing, if not wisdom,
at least a beastly friendliness
that makes me want to tell him
my secrets.

But that's not worship.
I've never asked the squirrel
where the glasses are.
I've never, like Hal,
dropped to my knees before him.
Never.

Our Life in Pennsylvania:
   Questions and Answers

Q: Where would we be, Nancy, if not for your ability to organize and think clearly?
A: In Pennsylvania.

Q: What would our life have been like if we had gone to Guatemala instead of Bolivia?
A: You would have become a first-rate auto mechanic.

Q: Where would we be now if we hadn't married?
A: In Pennsylvania.

Q: What would our life have been like without David and Kristin?
A: We would have had Fred and Agnes instead and they both would have rebelled. We would be miserable.

Q: What if I had fallen off that cliff on the Oregon coast?
A: You'd be dead.

Q: What if I didn't have music in my life? Where would I be without my French horn?
A: You'd be a rock collector in Pennsylvania. You'd enjoy listening to the rocks tumble. You'd make necklaces and bracelets.

Q: What if we didn't have Jesus?
A: Our life in Pennsylvania would be meaningless.

The List of Perils Grows

This isn't where I'm supposed to be,
he said, surfacing at the wrong end of the pool.
But the bottom is painted blue,
and the sides curve. I scraped my chin.
Curved blue bottoms disorient me.

We live in perilous times.
To the growing list—
    global warming,
    nuclear proliferation,
    la niña,
    triglycerides,
    pandemic—
now add this—

    curved blue bottoms.

My Husband Compliments Me

Nancy, you've told me that I
don't complain very much,
but I want you to know that you
don't complain a whole lot more
than I don't complain.

A Reassurance to My Husband
Who Sometimes Gets Kicked in Bed

While my feet may be
killing me, a sadistic
rebellion of body parts,
don't worry. My feet,
or any of my appendages
for that matter,
would never even dream
of harming you.

A Comment to My Husband
Who Tends to Let His Yes Be Yes and His No, No

You're too much of a literalist.
You take everything I say
and believe it.

Andrea

When my grandson was four-years-old,
he explained the Trinity to me,
what he had gleaned from Sunday school
and the Bible stories his mother read to him.
He told me the Trinity meant
the Father, his Son, and Andy.
Who? Andy, he repeated.
Before the greatest mystery of theology,
this little boy was not confused,
now that he had the names.
I was confused. The Spirit
had always seemed the most elusive
member of the holy threesome.
Dove. Wind. Breath. Water.
Hard to relate to.
Days later I overhead my grandson
singing one of the hymns
he had learned in that Sunday school.
As he sang the chorus in his still baby voice,
I finally got it. He sang,
Andy walks with me. Andy talks with me.
Andy tells me I am his own.
Of course. Spirit is God-up-close.
God who walks by my side.
Who tells me secrets.

I've never been drawn to call her Andy.
But in the early morning hours,
as I sit in my chair by the window,
I sometimes whisper, "Sister. Mother.
Best friend. Yes, yes, yes."
Sometimes I call her Andrea.
I sense her smile.

God and Cats

(Peter ponders)

I sometimes wonder, Grandma,
what gave God the idea
to make cats.

Why these self-centered
stripey patterned
fur-balls?

What made God
have the idea
to make cats?

Maybe he made them
to control against
over-population of mice
who, without cats,
might take over the world.

Maybe he had the idea
to make cats just
for our pleasure.

I wonder sometimes
about God and cats.

   [Peter, 10 years old]

Peter Wonders about Death and Other Stuff

Imagine what you would feel like
if you did not exist.

*****

What would you feel like if you were dead?
Would you still feel like you were there?
But how could you feel if you did not exist?
It's hard to explain.

*****

If you and Grandpa had not married,
would I have been born to strangers?
Or, if you and Grandpa had not married,
would I have been born at all?
Would I exist?

*****

If you're dead, you're gone.
What would you feel like if you were gone?
Would you think or have feelings?
It's so hard to explain.
I don't think you understand
what I'm trying to say, Grandma.

*****

If there was nothing when God didn't yet create the world,
how would you be there?
If you weren't born yet,
how would you be there?

Imagine not being there
and not being able to think.
It's not possible 'cause nothing can change that.
You would still be able to think and stuff.
It's just weird.

*****

No one knows what if feels like to be dead
because when you're dead you can't come back and tell
   people.

*****

I started to think about this since kindergarten.
When I think really really big,
my brain hurts.

*****

I've got a huge suggestion for the Bible:
They should make it easier to understand.

*****

The smallest word with the most complex meaning
is God.

>   *[Peter, 10 years old]*

Trout Tickling

Little Florence learned about trout tickling
from her uncle, learned to lie quietly on the bank
as an unsuspecting fish lurked in the shadows.
Slowly she lowered her hand, centimeter by centimeter.
She was a gentle soul and with great patience
she touched the fish's belly, began to stroke,
lulled it to trance. At the right moment
little Florence lifted her victim up
set him on the grass.
The trout twitched, shedding rainbows,
gasped, and eventually expired.
Much later Florence grew up
and married a large, gruff man.
Not given to sports, her husband excelled
at argument, poetry, and the telling
of strange stories.
It appears unlikely that Florence
ever learned to lull him to peace
by any means, never got him
up on the grass. In that marriage,
the only one gasping for air
was Florence herself.

> *[Grevel Lindop in his biography,* Charles Williams: The Third Inkling, *writes about Williams's wife, Florence, as a little girl learning the skill of trout-tickling from her uncle.]*

No Survivors
Joshua 10:40

In terrible obedience
Joshua subdued the land—
    hill country
    the Negev
    western foothills
    mountain slopes,
together with the kings.
The target, by holy command—
any being that breathed.
No beast, no baby escaped
the brutal blitz.
A challenge, yes, but
not too hard for a band
of soldiers seasoned to kill,
not nearly as hard
as God's latter command
to warriors of a new regime—
love your enemies.

This time, God,
you go too far.

Old Testament War Revised

As a sophomore
our daughter made the coveted
cheerleading squad.
Some of the chants underscored
the brutality of high school sports.
One afternoon, I watched
as the girls waved their pom-poms,
danced, leaped, and led
the crowd in
   Kill kill
   Hate hate
   Murder murder
   Mutilate
   Go, Team!
I was glad when the school
year ended.

The Wedding Gift
1 Kings 9:16-17

Not satisfied with the usual—
sheets, cookware, even
a frilly nightgown or two—
Pharoah attacked the town of Gezer,
killed all the people, burnt it to the ground,
then presented it to his daughter
as a wedding gift.
I can hardly imagine her reaction.
Gee, thanks, Pop.
To appease his new wife
and keep up good relations
with his powerful father-in-law,
Solomon rebuilt the town.
It's doubtful the princess
ever visited.

Course Correction?

Psalm 130:19-24

David declared his hatred
for your enemies, God,
suggested you kill them all.
He followed this declaration
by asking that you search his heart
for any offensive way
and lead him in your paths.
Did you do it, God?
Did you give him a preview
of your upside-down kingdom?
As an old man, did David
bless his enemies?
Did he love them?

What?
Psalm 133

Take the idea of unity.
How good and pleasant, says the psalmist.
He should have added the word *rare.*
The ideal is sweet;
the reality can be bitter.

While our denomination is no longer
together, a few friendly bridges have been built.
I guess unity can happen within limits.

And then there's that stuff about precious oil.
A little too precious. Poured in the hair?
Running down the face? Gumming up the beard?
Was this some kind of ancient beauty treatment?
Is this the way fellowship is supposed to feel?
Sticky? Gummy? Hard to clean up?
No wonder it's so rare.

Strangely Appropriate
Luke 2:1-6

Joseph had no way to make advance reservations,
so of course the inn was full with the surge
of humanity in town for the census.
The harassed innkeeper was a kind man
and felt for the plight of the young couple, about
to become a family. The provision of his manger
was makeshift but all he had to give.
It must have been crowded with the beasts
of the extra guests. It probably needed
to be mucked out and fresh straw supplied,
but who had time for all that, what with
the demands of his clientele, all of them stressed,
tired, and hungry? So Joseph and Mary
made do, relieved at any shelter
for the birth coming way too soon.
Similar to sleeping under a bridge
or on a park bench, it was perhaps made
a little warmer with the breath of beasts.
Inconvenient by any standards, it was a strangely
appropriate beginning for one
who would give his life for people
sleeping under bridges or on park benches.

CEO
Luke 9:28-36

Peter, impulsive, full
of good ideas,
only-trying-to-help,
offered to organize the occasion.
The voice from the cloud
didn't reprimand him,
didn't say, *Be quiet, Peter.*
It said simply, *Listen to Jesus.*
Many Peters still offer
their skills and advice.
The voice gives the same answer.

Little Children Know

Revealed to little children. –Luke 10:21

I've been in school
since I was five years old.
I wrote a dissertation,
for heaven's sake!
And read more books
than I care to count.
All of it for heaven's sake.
Yet sometimes I pace,
ponder theological
contradictions,
and ask God,
What's it all about?
Then my four-year-old
grandson sings me a song.
He tells me,

> *Jesus loves me, this I know*
> *for the Bible tells me so.*

I sit back and smile.

Such Friends

Use worldly wealth to gain friends for yourself.
   –Jesus, Luke 16:6

If I could I'd invite you
to stay in my beach condo
for free. You could even use my yacht.
Help yourself to my wine
cellar any time you want.
Burdensome debts? I'll cover them.
Impossible dreams? I've got it.

However, my precarious economic
state outweighs my generosity,
so I get it why you don't like me.
I understand perfectly
why I don't have any friends.

Verbal Rewards

Luke 17:7-10

Is that all the thanks I get?
is a question the disciple
never asks.

Saint Paul Meets a Quaker Lady

Women should remain silent in the churches.
  –1 Corinthians 14:34

In the fullness of personal time,
1992 to be exact, the Friends Church
recorded me as a minister of the gospel.
It recognized my call to public ministry,
and the gathered body affirmed me publicly.
I thanked them all, but what I didn't tell them
was my sense that St. Paul himself
had joined us. He was standing in back,
on the left side of the meeting house
by the rack of theological pamphlets.
He was clapping.
He was grinning from ear to ear.

Clay Pot

> *We have this treasure in jars of clay.*
> *–2 Corinthians 4:6-7*

Years ago an enemy turned friend
gave us a gift, a clay pot
he had discovered in an Incan burial mound.
The rough texture and rounded bottom
gave evidence to its antiquity.
It was crafted to nestle in the dirt.
My anthropologist husband
recognized its value,
not only as a cultural artifact,
but as a symbol of friendship.
Its roundness meant it couldn't sit
on our shelf without support,
so we placed it in a bowl.
One evening as we were horsing around,
we accidently knocked it off the shelf
and with alarm watched it break
into pieces. Distressed
more for the sake of the friendship
than for the loss of the artifact,
we determined to mend it.
We spread the pieces out on the table,
a complicated jigsaw puzzle, and began
figuring out where each one belonged.
Little by little, over the course
of several weeks, we glued the pot
back to wholeness. Miraculously,
it held together,
but we could do nothing to hide
the cracks that crisscrossed its surface.

Our friend appreciated the effort,
didn't mind the imperfections.
The accident and its aftermath
sealed our relationship.
Now, when we place a candle
in the pot, it's the cracks
that let the light shine through.

Just Asking
Ephesians 4:1-3

Was it optimistic naiveté
when Paul told the children of God
to *make every effort*
to keep the unity of the Spirit
in the bond of peace?
Church history suggests that.
More than geography
and the accidents of birth
have divided the body
of Christ. While Jesus
responded with silence
to Pilate's question,
What is truth?,
the church has squabbled,
split, and splintered its multitudinous
answers down through
the centuries. Even we Quakers
in the northwest corner
of a country once known
for its open arms
have sacrificed our reputation
as people of peace
and made every effort
to propound our separate versions
of gospel truth. Now, victims all
of the resulting divorce,
we seek revival and hope
to once again walk
worthy of our calling.
Have mercy on us all.

Offensive

Philippians 2:1-4

Value others above yourselves, Paul writes. *Be humble.*
I'm drawn to that teaching, but I have questions.
Is this in reference to differences
in a local congregation, an instruction to respectfully
   listen
to our sisters and brothers in the body of Christ?
Does it also mean I need to deem the political views
of my relatives as worthy of consideration as my own?
How am I to see Muslims, Hindus, Buddhists,
animists, liberals, atheists, and the multitude of people
who follow other ways? How am I—a missionary,
for heaven's sake!—to value these others
while at the same time affirming
that the name of Jesus is above all names,
that one day *every knee will bow, every tongue confess
that Jesus Christ is Lord*?
How do I respect others while telling them,
You're wrong. I'm right. Repent and believe.
I am drawn to tolerance, not proclamation.
Maybe that's why I'm not a good evangelist.
God, help me.

A Word from Grandma
1 Timothy 5:3-4

Okay, you kids and grandkids.
Listen to what the man says.
Even though I'm not a widow,
I'm old. Your first and most
emphatically religious obligation
is to be really really really nice
to me.

Trail Guide
2 John

First off, take the right trail,
the one with the triple name—
Truth, Obedience, Love.
Easy to remember. Hard to hike.
Second, keep on the path.
Side tracks and animal prints
will entice. Ignore them.
Those far dark trees
harbor beasts
and the air is foul.
Third, equip yourselves
with the basics—a good walking
stick, water, shoes with traction.
There are rocks ahead, fallen limbs,
crevices, and narrow ledges.
Fourth, slow and steady does it.
Fifth, stay together.
Your hiking buddies
will keep you moving
and occasionally make you smile.
Sixth, sing as you go.
Enjoy the scenery.
Laugh at the mockingbirds.
Follow these instructions
and in good time
you'll arrive.

Life in an
Old Growth Forest

Are We Old Yet?

he asked me
and I couldn't answer him.
Old? Is there a line in time
called "old" where one day
you're not there
and the next you cross over
and you're in?
I don't know.
It's all strange territory.

"The Golden Years," it's called,
second childhood, maturity,
the third stage of life, retirement,
or the Spanish version, jubilee.
The experts (who are here, there,
and everywhere) tell us
there are three stages:
young old age, middle old age,
and old old age.
I guess that's helpful.

So where are we?

Something inside tells me
that when we stop asking silly questions
we will have arrived.
But without the questions
how will we know where we are?

In the meantime, as long as
our legs hold us upright
and our eyes and ears
are somewhat operational,
we'll just keep on walking,
looking around, listening,
and asking questions.
Are we old yet?

Who Done It?

Last night someone's dog pooped
on the carpet in the hall.
In the morning the unseemly little pile
was still there.
Who did it? Was it Nils or Samantha?
Or did Niko from the fourth floor
come up to visit and leave his calling card?
The forest floor is becoming
a little more biodiverse
than any of us want.

Old Romance

The trees talk.
Leaves seem to whisper and
below the understory
swimming from root to root
a vast fungal network
channels messages of danger,
drought, and radical change.
Between species
across the miles
the unspoken word goes forth.

Don't think you can keep it secret.
This particular forest has many leaves
all fluttering in the least rumored breeze.
Deep underground
the mushrooms are on the move.

Told to Me at Lunch

When my husband was dying, she told me,
he asked if I believed in reincarnation.
I observed that it seemed to be part
of many world religions.
He replied, *When you follow me
in death and we meet in some reincarnated state,
will you spend another lifetime with me?*
What if I die first? I responded.
He frowned, poked a finger in my rib cage,
and growled, *You won't. I forbid it.*

Unacquainted

My friend Harriet
tells me that her son
visited her soon after he died.
He came and sat on the edge
of her bed. He spoke no
words, but his presence
comforted. When Harriet reached
up and turned on the light,
no one was there.
But she knew what she knew.
He was, she says, *unacquainted
with the limits of death.*

Tact

My friend Sarah
just had a colonoscopy.
At the end
the young doctor told her,
*We don't usually do colonoscopies
on people as old as you.*
He went on,
*Any polyps you have
will take about ten years
to become cancerous,
and by then
you'll be dead.*

Over by the Creek

Sam's wife died last year. He's only been here
since January. That's a lot of adjusting to do.
Every morning he's down in the exercise room,
walking slowly but consistently on the treadmill,
his way of choosing life. Now in his mid-90s,
his PhD in medical research helps him scan
his neighbors, make wise diagnoses,
which he wisely keeps to himself.
But his lifelong research in giardia doesn't
contribute much to life in this place. It's too clean here.
I can appreciate his work, though, having wrestled
with the beasts myself. I feel a little safer
knowing there's an ancient giardia specialist
who lives just over by the creek.

[Sam's neighborhood in the home is known as Creekside.]

Skimpy Blessing

Have a super-duper day! he called
as he walked out of the gym,
having completed his morning discipline
of temple maintenance.
I don't remember my response,
probably something like, *You, too,*
as I continued to chug away,
arms and legs rotating,
cool air from the open window
mitigating the sweat on my forehead.
I considered the generosity of his blessing,
compared it to what I would have said
if I had left first: *Have a good day.*
Seems sort of skimpy. A good day.
But, on the other hand, good is,
well, *good.* And it seems to be
getting gooder all the time.
So I will accept the friendly effusiveness
of super-duper
(after all, it makes me smile)
and continue to proffer my homespun version.

Have a good day, Brian.

Three Conversations in the Exercise Room

1. City Chicken

We had city chicken for our Christmas dinner. It's a family favorite. Can any of you tell me what it is?

Does it have to do with where you eat it?

Nope.

Is it spiced with obscure herbs and served with tofu or something weird like that?

Nope. It's skewered pieces of pork loin, oven baked in a cast iron skillet. It comes from the Ohio Valley.

Why that name?

Don't know. It's always been called city chicken. That's just the way it is.

2. The Old Folks Do a Post-Christmas Spring Cleaning

We cleaned our oven yesterday. It's a Whirlpool and the manual says 'self-cleaning.' In quotation marks.

Was it? Self-cleaning?

Well. At the end of the day Carol told me she'd give up our trip to Hawaii if we would buy a new stove.

Are you gonna do it?

I'm thinking about it. Makes sense. My knees don't like it when I'm down on the floor scraping the oven with a knife.

I washed out our cupboards yesterday. Any mice we have will be mighty disappointed.

We've never done that in all our years of marriage!

I'm gonna clean the refrigerator today.

That's funny. So am I.

Let's have a potluck tonight. Bring together all our green leftovers.

Sounds like fun. Grim, but fun.

3. In the Dead of Winter

Why do they call this time 'the dead of winter'? No one ever mentions 'the dead of spring' in April.

Or 'the dead of summer' in July.

Maybe we're all just 'dead to rights,' whatever that means.

What does it mean? I've never heard that phrase.

I have, but I don't know what it means either.

Here. I'll look it up on my iPhone. . . . 'Dead to rights'—It comes from the underworld of the mid-nineteenth century—the mob—and means 'caught in the act.'

Conclusion of the Matter

What was he doing and how did he get caught?

He was foolishly stealing a Whirlpool oven. He was caught by the city chickens. In the dead of winter.

Goodbye

I'm having my waterfalls
removed. It will be good
when all the mist
that floats between me
and the sun is gone. But,
even so, I'm going to miss
the rush and swirl of moving
water, the mad leap over the edge,
the plunge and crash and all
the lovely daily drama that goes
with having my very own
waterfalls somewhere
inside my head.

>   *[Note: the word "cataract" can refer to the clouding of the eye's lens or to a waterfall.]*

Hal, at 76

Instead of
> *whistle while you work,*

it's now
> *mutter while you putter.*

In that Very Instant

I was startled this morning
to see a strange old woman
staring at me from the bathroom mirror.
Who is she? How did she get here?
Should I pull the emergency cord
by the toilet? Am I safe?
Such white hair!
Those lines around the eyes!
Those spots! Poor thing.
Even as I pitied her,
something about the pathetic look
she gave me back made me laugh.
In that very instant, I recognized
her, accepted her, and loved her back.
Just as she is.

How I Am

Sometimes I am firm,
resolute, and strong.
I say what I mean
and I mean what I say.
Other times, given my age,
I sort of tend to be wishy-washy.
I do, absolutely, remember
a time several years ago
when I impressed myself
at how decisive I was.
I enjoyed the feeling
and determined to feel that
firmness of character
again in the future.
And I will. I'm almost
certain of it.

A Brief Poetic Treatise on Fine Cuisine

I am a fan of the HITO method
of cooking, an ancient tradition
passed down through the lineage
of the Forsythe family
and graciously lived out
in my sainted mother's kitchen.
Now it's my turn
to pass it on to you.
In essence, you open your cupboards
and your refrigerator, then thoughtfully
peruse the contents.
No busy running to multiple gourmet stores,
no searching to procure weird tropical spices,
no profligate spending of your hard-earned pennies.
Just take what you have on hand,
mix it together, and
Hope It Turns Out. HITO.
It usually does.

It Had To Be Done

Seated behind my hard
wood executive desk,
looking down
on the city below,
I finally did
what had to be done.
I invited all my mental
neurons in and I told them,
*Guys, you've been doing
a great job, but times
are tough, and I have
to let you go.*
I fired them all.

> *[Inspired by a poster for an online class
> on brain exercises for the elderly,
> guaranteed to fire our mental neurons.]*

Just a Tweak

> Yes, Lord. It's me again,
> here in this new day.

Good morning, dear one. Well come.
What can I do for you today?

> Thanks for asking. (Even though
> you already know the answer,
> your courtesy encourages me.)
> And thank you for this awesome
> body/mind/spirit.
> I am wonder-full at how
> wonderfully and fearfully
> I am made.
>
> But since you asked,
> could you just tweak
> this body a little?
> I know I'm growing older
> and that a bit of wear 'n tear is natural,
> but is this particular malfunction
> really necessary?
> Just a tweak, God. That's all I'm asking.
> You can do it if you want to.

I want.

> Okay, then. That's what I'm asking for.
> Here, let me sing my prayer to you.
>
>> Have mercy on me and heal me.
>> Set my feet upon a rock.
>> Put a new song in my heart.
>> O Lord, have mercy on me.

*Okay. But you'll have to let me do this
my way, in my time.*

    Yes, God. My times are in your hands.
    I'll wait.
    And in the meantime,
    I thank you for your grace
    and your artistry in making me.
    And I anticipate
    the tweak.

    Amen

At the Beginning
of Another Grim Day

I lean in to hear
what the Spirit says.
She tells me
that my task is to
    -be kind to myself
    -be kind to Hal
    -pick one other person
and be kind

*She who has ears to hear
let her hear,* the Spirit says.
She goes on, tells me to
    -notice things
    -make a list
    -say thank you

Next she tells me to
remember those people
who irritate me.
Imagine being kind
to them.

Finally she tells me to
write a silly poem,
a really really silly poem.
(Could this be it?)

*If you have ears to hear,
then hear,* she says again,

'cause this is all *Big Stuff.*

Over the River and through the Woods
    Psalm 90:1

to Grandmother's house we go.
We used to sing that at Thanksgiving.
My mind gobbled up the image,
an idealized Thomas Kincaid calendar picture
complete with snow, a horse-drawn sleigh,
candle-light streaming from the windows,
and a plump, rosy-cheeked grandma,
apple pie in hand, waiting to welcome
the family home. I knew that's how it would be
when I became an old lady. Grandpa and I
would be the hub of a living wheel
of hugs and stories, music and good food.
Welcome, welcome! Welcome home!

That's not how it turned out.
We are well taken care of in our retirement home,
but our small apartment can host two or three
at the most. Family gatherings take place
at one of our kids' homes and now include
numerous in-laws. We have to decide where
to go for Thanksgiving dinner. Thomas Kincaid
flew out the window years ago.

Thank you for replacing my fantasy
with a vision of reality richer and warmer
than any calendar picture.
You, Lord, have been our dwelling place
through all generations.
You are the hub of the wheel.
You shelter us, feed us, teach and discipline us, give us rest.
You make us one in you.
You're the one who says, *Welcome home.*

Crowded, but Green
Psalm 92:12-15

It's getting close
in these two rooms
what with two full-grown
trees, him—a cedar,
me—a palm.
Originally from two
different climes,
we've blended and now
get along well. Our roots
go through the floor,
possibly with consequences
to the people living below
us, but they don't complain.
Our branches reach toward
the sun streaming through
the windows. They intertwine.
Fruit litters the floor,
manages to stay fresh, ready
for consumption. Our color
scheme is all shades of green
with pops of red, yellow, and orange.
Yes, the rooms are crowded,
but the scent is delicious,
and the air clean, wholesome,
and full of light.

Bird-napping: The Secret of Old Age

Deuteronomy 22:6-7

Once as I was walking back from the creek
I heard a chirpy commotion low to the ground.
I followed the sound to a bush next to the wall
where a robin was feeding three noisy infants.
They crowded the nest and seemed to be competing,
beaks wide open, for whatever their mother
was offering. When Momma Bird became aware
of my face just one foot from her face
she escaped out the opposite end of the bush,
flew off some twenty feet and landed on the path ahead.
She stood there watching as her offspring
kept up their insistent chorus. According to Moses,
if I had reached in and appropriated that nest
with its burden of birds, taken it
back to my room to study and nourish,
leaving the mother bereft of her young,
the rest of my life would be prosperous and long.
Even so, I relinquished the opportunity, left
the angry birds to their mother. When I returned
the next day, the nest was empty. I hope
they survived. I wish them all a long and happy
bird life, whatever happens to mine.

Ancient Blessing
Luke 2:21-38; Psalm 92:12-15

Old people have a reputation
for wisdom, but that's often
not the reality. Alzheimer's,
dementia, or outright crankiness
can overcome personality in the aged.
In spite of that,
sometimes we are blessed
to know the green leaves
of an ancient tree, taste fruit
that sweetens with the years.
So with Simeon and Anna.
Faithful servants, approaching
death, both lingered on
in the hope of his coming.
Years of waiting met reward
in the courts of the temple.
Filled with joy, held by the child
they held in their arms,
they thanked God, blessed the babe
and his parents, and gave public
witness that has become
a permanent part of the story.
Thank God for the legacy
of such as Simeon and Anna.

The Temple Ages
1 Corinthians 6:19

I wonder about the fitness
of this temple. Is it adequate
for holy occupation?
The foundations have neuropathy
and the two extensions creak
with arthritis. A miasma
of exhaustion often fills
the inner chamber and the outer
shell shows some cracking.
Still I manage to keep it clean
and swept. The high windows
look to the mountains, let in light.
The belfry is free of cobwebs.
So, come, Holy Spirit.
Inhabit your home.

Devotions

I take my imagination
between my two hands
and slowly pull,
stretch it thin thin thin
then just before it snaps,
I let go, jump back,
and glimpse the face of God.

In the Fullness of Time

It seems like years
I've been living in skinny time
long and thin and transparent.
The view of the other side
waves and wrinkles
like cellophane
like looking through dusty lenses.
It stretches out.
Thirsty, I cup my hands
but the water slips through.
Nothing stays.
That's all about to change.
Little by little
then bunch by bunch
time will thicken
grow solid.
When the cold comes
I will ice skate.
The surface will hold.
The sky will clear.
The trees on the far shore
will welcome me home.

Title Index

A

A Brief Poetic Treatise on Fine Cuisine 99
A Comment to My Husband Who Tends to
   Let His Yes Be Yes and His No, No 63
American Monsters 50
Ancient Blessing 107
Andrea 64
A Quaker Lady Learns to Swear 27
A Reassurance to My Husband
   Who Sometimes Gets Kicked in Bed 63
Are We Old Yet? 86
A Tale of Two Cows 31
At the Beginning
   of Another Grim Day 103
A Whole Nother 28
A Word from Grandma 83
A Word Like *Lugubrious* 18

B

Bare Naked 44
Bilingualism 29
Bird-napping: The Secret of Old Age 106
Body Shop: Parts and Replacements 56

C

CEO 75
Challenged 29
Clay Pot 79
Come to Your Senses, Nancy 33
Course Correction? 72
Crowded, but Green 105

D

Devotions 108

E

Eating My Words 43

F

Fat Chance 45
Food for Thought 49

G

God and Cats 65
God's Poem 35
Going Dutch 46
Goodbye 96
Grammatical Violence 28

H

How I Am 98

I

I'm Good with Languages 17
In Answer to Your Question 48
In that Very Instant 97
In the Fullness of Time 109
In the Nick of Time 55
It Had To Be Done 100

J

Just Asking 81
Just a Tweak 101

L

Little Children Know 76

M

Medical Breakthrough 52
My Bad 49
My Husband Compliments Me 63

N

No Experts at Home Here 22
No Survivors 69

O

Odebolt 30
Offensive 82
Old Romance 88
Old Testament War Revised 70
Our Life in Pennsylvania:
    Questions and Answers 61
Over by the Creek 91
Over the River and through the Woods 104

P

    Peter Wonders about Death and Other Stuff 66

Q

    Qualms 24

S

    Seven Views of a Rabbit Trail 57
    Short Poems on Particle Physics 20
    Skimpy Blessing 92
    Sometimes Understatement Doesn't Work 39
    Strangely Appropriate 74
    Such Friends 77

T

    Tact 90
    The Creeps 25
    The List of Perils Grows 62
    The Mature Poet Takes a Walk in the Woods 32
    The Naked Eye 47
    The Pregnant Pause 44
    There Were Five of Them 54
    The Temple Ages 108
    The Turnip 53
    The Ultimate Bull 26
    The Wedding Gift 71
    Three Conversations in the Exercise Room 93
    Told to Me at Lunch 89
    Trail Guide 84
    Trout Tickling 68

U

    Unacquainted 89
    Uncertain Terms 42

V

    Verbal Rewards 78

W

    What? 73
    Who Done It? 88
    Why I Never Use the Word *Plethora* 19
    With a Name like Weasel 23
    Worshipping the Squirrel 60

Y

    You Have a Way with Words 16

First Line Index

A

Although a Quaker 28
As a sophomore 70
As I walked in the room 60

B

Be wary of the exclamation point 39

D

David declared his hatred 72

F

First off, take the right trail 84

G

Grandma, she told me 16

H

Have a super-duper day! he called 92
he asked me 86
Here's good news for all 52

he says 33
hesitates before opening the door 44
how could he not 23

I

I am a fan of the HITO method 99
I am linguistically challenged 29
If I could I'd invite you 77
If it doesn't pan out exactly 43
If I tease someone in English 29
If you can believe that 35
If you're going to give me a nother 28
I lean in to hear 103
I left my coat 47
Imagine what you would feel like 66
I'm having my waterfalls 96
I'm told that fish is brain food 49
I never met a tarsal 22
In terrible obedience 69
in the beginning 54
In the fullness of personal time 78
is a provocative name 44
I shouldn't have said anything 49
I sometimes wonder, Grandma 65
I spent the years of my infancy and childhood 30
Is that all the thanks I get? 78
I stood at the window last evening 31
I take my imagination 108
It's an American secret 56
It seems like years 109
It's getting close 105
It wasn't very appetizing, so 53
It wears rhinestone earrings 19
I've been in school 76

I've been known to take 45
I was a believer. I grew up 55
I was startled this morning 97
I will continue to say 42
I wonder about the fitness 108

J

Joseph had no way to
   make advance reservations 74

L

Last night someone's dog pooped 88
Let's go Dutch, he said 46
Little Florence learned about trout tickling 68

M

My friend Harriet 89
My friend Sarah 90

N

Nancy, you've told me that I 63
needs a poem of its own 18
Not satisfied with the usual 71

O

Okay, you kids and grandkids 83
Old people have a reputation 107
Once as I was walking back from the creek 106
on hearing my grandson complain 22

P

Peter, impulsive, full 75
Please, whatever you say 22

Q

Q: Where would we be, Nancy,
    if not for your ability 61

S

Sam's wife died last year. He's only been here 91
Seated behind my hard 100
Sometimes I am firm 98
Sometimes the path you were following 57
Stiff but receptive, they wait for the rustling 50

T

Take the idea of unity 73
Take the neutrino 20
The trees talk 88
This isn't where I'm supposed to be 62
This meat came 26
This morning on the path to the beach 17
to Grandmother's house we go 104

V

Value others above yourselves,
    Paul writes. *Be humble* 82

W

Was it optimistic naivety 81
We had city chicken for our Christmas dinner.
    It's a family 93
Whenever he appears on the screen 25
When my grandson was four-years-old 64
When my husband was dying, she told me 89
While my feet may be 63
While poor in the goods 24
Whose woods these are 32

Y

Years ago an enemy turned friend 79
Yes, I used to put God 48
Yes, Lord. It's me again 101
You need to learn to swear 27
You're too much of a literalist 63

www.ingramcontent.com/pod-product-compliance
Lightning Source LLC
Chambersburg PA
CBHW010045090426
42735CB00020B/3399